COURT NAMING
CONVENTIONS

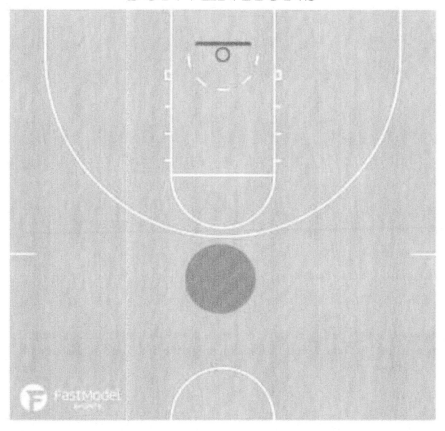

"Top of the key" is one of the maximum essential locations withinside the courtroom docket, the spot is secure due to the fact it's miles a ways farfar from sidelines and baseline/1/2 of courtroom docket and trapping is hard. Most groups begin their offense here. Good connection to High publish , and wings. Perfect vicinity to play excessive ball display.

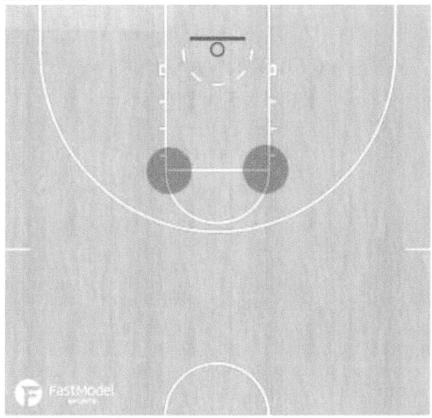

Elbow is a high-quality vicinity for a mid-variety taking pictures and begin penetrating. In "horns" performs maximum of the time large men (four and 5) get those spots.

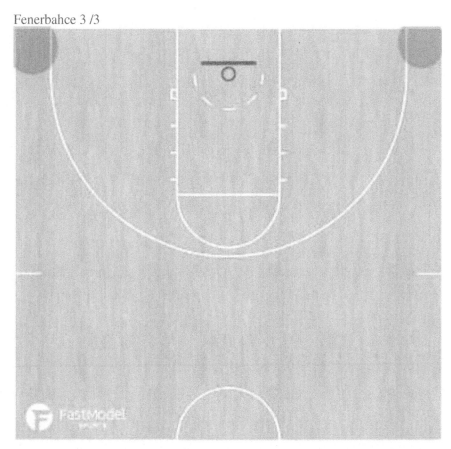

I suppose this spot is getting warmer and warmer each day. The 3 factor line isn't a semi-circle so there are distance differences. The closest distance to the rim for a 3 factor is the corners, that's why nook threes are so essential, greater correct and greater valuable. Help is continually coming from corners making nook gamers greater open.

Teaching factor : I strongly endorse the gamers to be very near the baseline in which even one foot gain is so essential for spacing these days. You will see maximum gamers rush and try and move excessive or reduce to the rim, hold them calm and lead them to live withinside the nook making them rating greater threes and
essential for spacing as well.

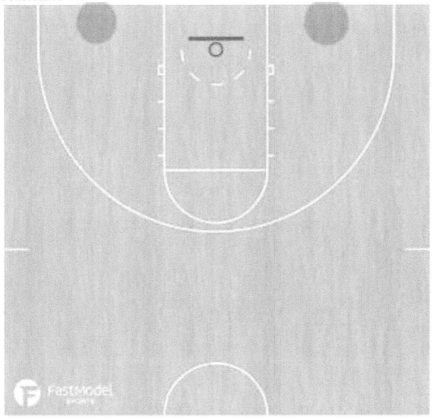

Hight publish and quick corners are very powerful towards sector defenses, can create layups, dunks. The cuts to the alternative of the power could make high-quality advantages. Also powerful vicinity to make displays for nook threes.

When I say nook display I am now no longer speaking approximately going for the fellow withinside the nook who has the ball. I suppose the worst factor for a ball display is the nook. What I changed into referring for this display is like : the third man withinside the 2-three sector, who's liable for protecting nook shots. Etc.

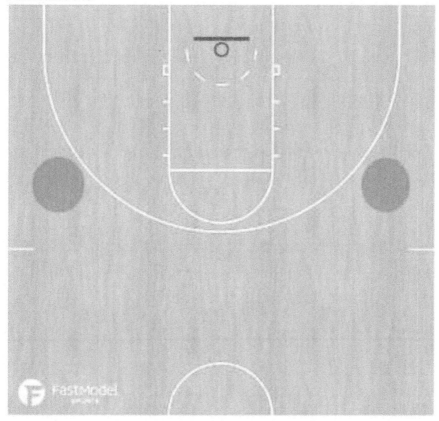

Forwards personal those spots. As I play ahead myself, I locate corners and wings appears like home.

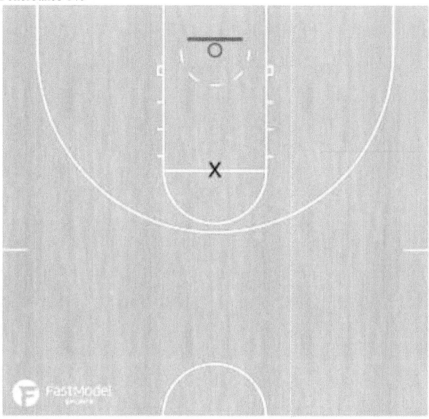

This is the spot in which you have to forestall your penetrations, make your "bounce to the balls". In NBA there are policies to keep away from staying here, however in FIBA you may continually cowl this vicinity and protect it. In Europe I don't suppose we've a call for this spot.

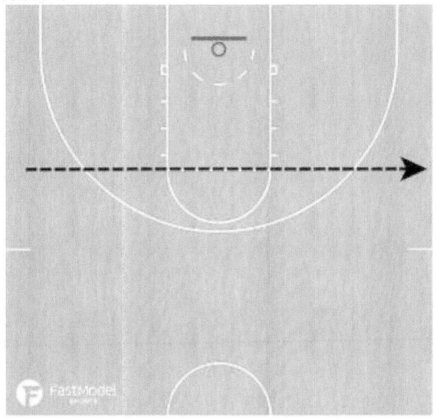

Great time period for in which your Forwards have to live, now no longer too deep now no longer too excessive. (relying on what you're gambling, my preferred spot for forwards continues to be the nook though.)

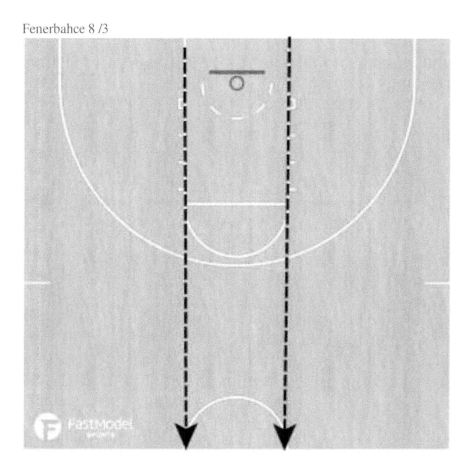

Another time period this is used to outline in which you need to position your gamers. Most of the time border on your gamers now no longer to byskip and now no longer to collide every other. Creating an opening among them for spacing

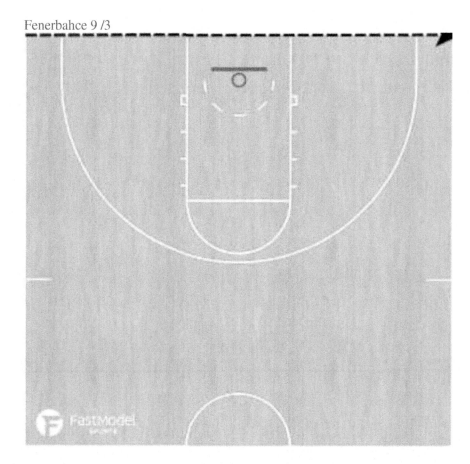

Your buddy in defense.

Teaching factor : inform your participant to step on the road to make certain now no longer be exceeded via way of means of the road..

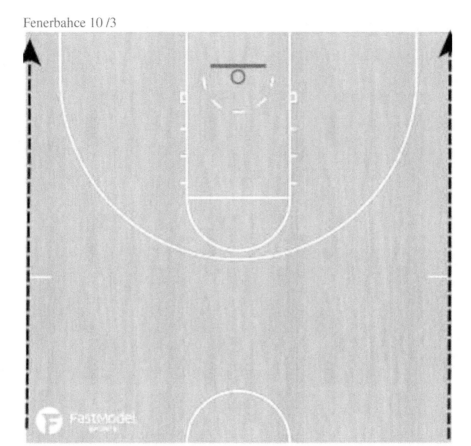

Another buddy of you at the same time as on defense.

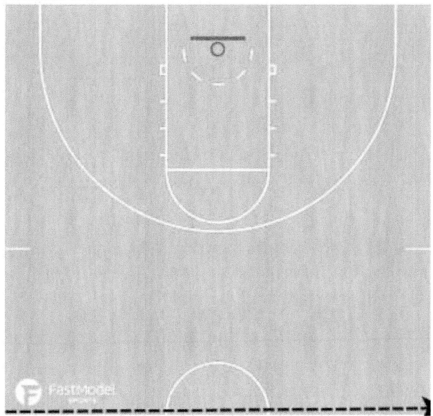

You have such a lot of friends !!!! Pressing the fellow who's passing proper this line would possibly paintings on newbies.

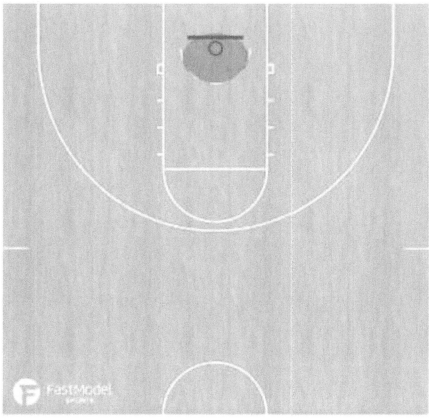

This is the final factor in which you have to be protecting 2-1 situations.

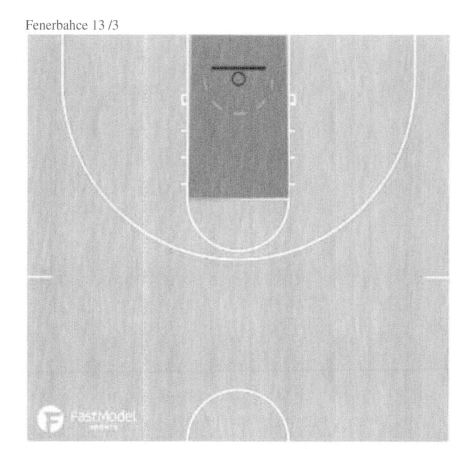

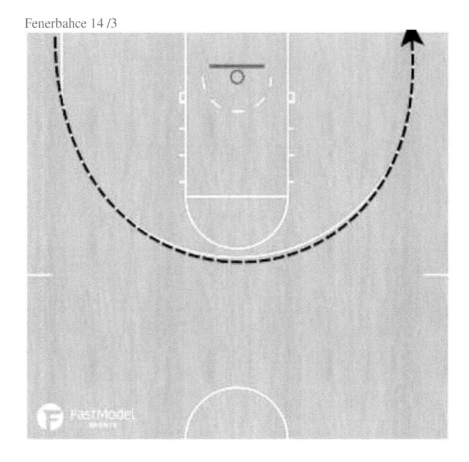

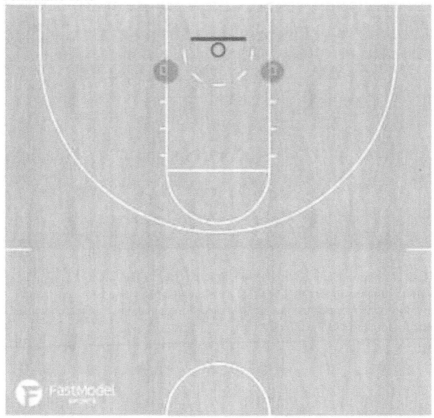

The sport is evolving from recommendations to a few recommendations however nonetheless you want to be appropriate withinside the low publish. Low publish performs can create high-quality earning as twos and additionally threes. If your private has a length gain use it, If you've got got a large, sized, gifted man, maximum probable there could be double groups, (a few groups near the baseline, a few groups near the center) appropriate ball motion can punish the ones helps.

Nowadays we see many guards gambling publish united states well, If I see a large length distinction I might endorse to position that man to this role to make the most it.

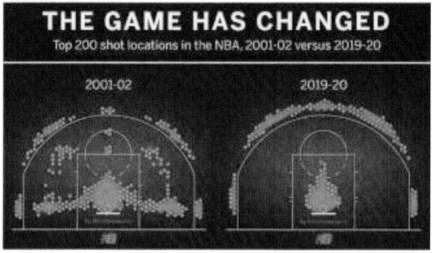

Here is a photo displaying the distinction of basketball evolving from mid-variety jumpers to threes. The satisfactory manner to attain is threes, layups and loose throws. For me the worst shot you may make is a in which you're one foot inner or at the 3 factor line.

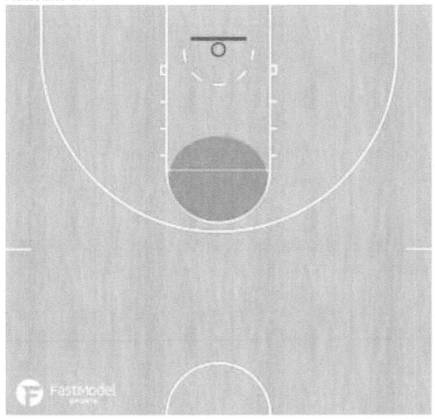

If there may be a private who can do mid-variety jumpers , it's miles nonetheless an awesome vicinity to apply it, additionally these days you may quick roll (Not rolling all of the manner to the rim) and you may locate the alternative men in the back of the three factor line, dispensing passes.

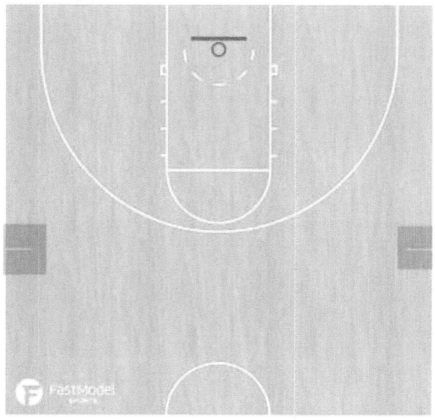

Know in which the ball gets be lower back in the sport, after a timeout or begin of a period. While drawing your set play it's miles very essential. After your final timeout, the sport will maximum probable will begin here.

The timeout rule has modified lately in FIBA. In the Last 2:00 of the sport, whilst you name a timeout (If the ball is on your courtroom docket) you may improve the ball to fighters 1/2 of courtroom docket and use 14 seconds or begin out of your courtroom docket and use 24 seconds.

CHART READING (XS AND OS)

When it's far approximately Xs and Os , what you draw must be understood through the gamers. As some distance as I apprehend the performs which might be drawn withinside the timeouts are already been practiced earlier than. It is simply reminding human beings what they must do. Might be a few exceptions for sure. Going with the practiced units makes extra experience to me on the beginning, trust me , even supposing Obradovic comes and attracts one of the excellent performs of him , your gamers will now no longer be capable of locate their spots withinside the courtroom docket.

When drawing units , please draw them as smooth to be apprehend and easy as viable. I am looking a few timeout movies and maximum of the time drawings are crap. Here is the Xs and Os drawing terminology.

I actually have visible a few coaches simply say we're going to run this (practiced play from their playbook), with out displaying it again. I suppose that's Chuck Norris cool. But I am continually at the visible side, can placed a few tweaks in step with your fighters tactics. The amazing coaches communicate approximately a couple of ownership in a timeout. Lets see how we draw to forums and what they mean.

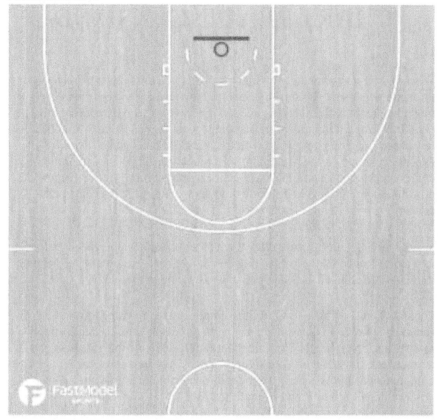

Your empty 1/2 of basketball courtroom docket and additionally your board will appear like this

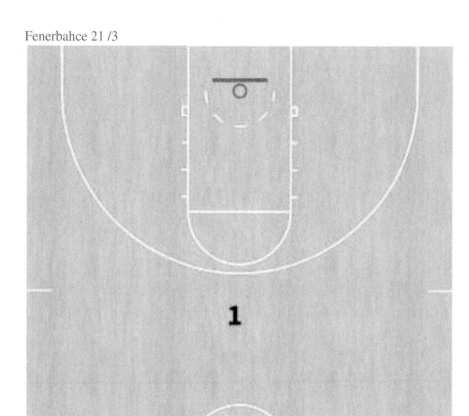

Adding your 1st participant , his call is John

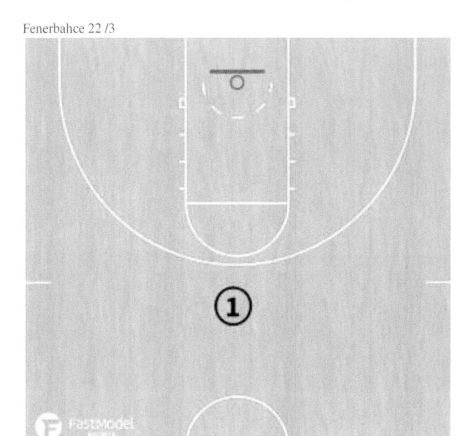

Giving the ball ownership to him now John has the ball

John dribbles to the left.

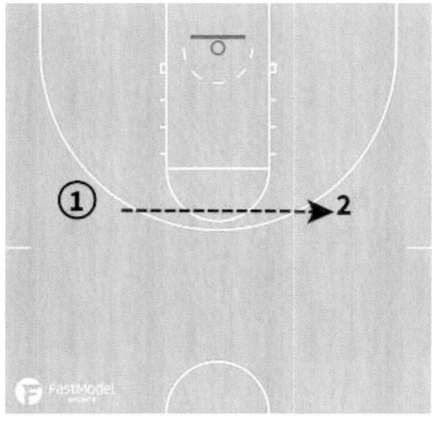

Then his group mate Eric comes and John passes to Eric

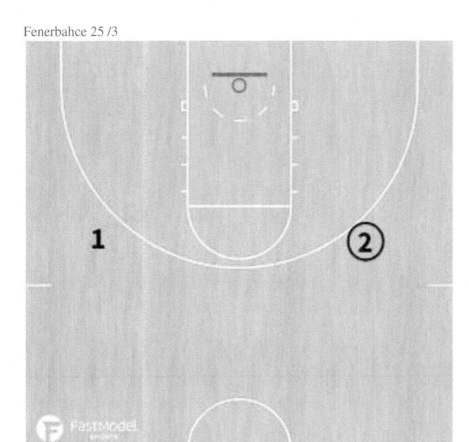

Now Eric has the ball

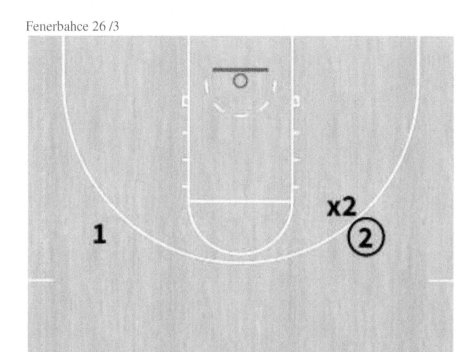

Then an opponent arrives and begins offevolved to shield Eric

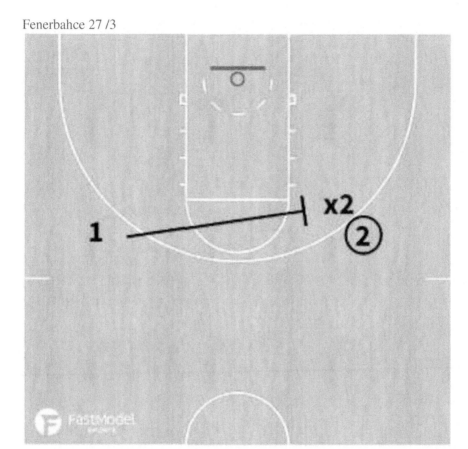

John runs towards Eric and makes a display screen

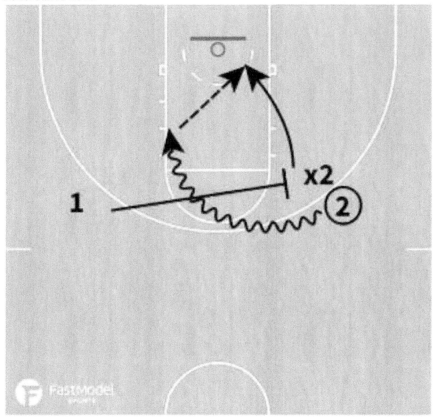

Eric dribbles the use of the display screen, John rolls and reduce in the direction of the rim (arrow) and Eric passes to him.

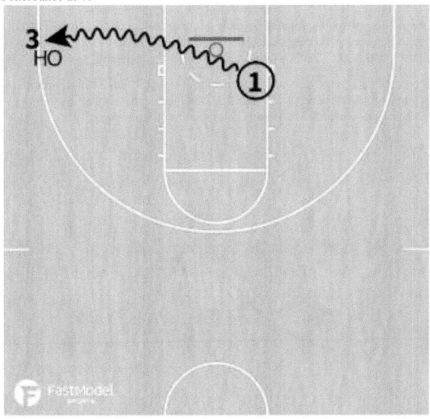

John receives the rebound and dribbles to his buddy Tom and offers the ball to him with out passing (handoff)

I actually have now no longer visible any charts for Handoffs , If I am drawing stay in a recreation state of affairs I especially say it's far an Handoff , If I want to attract it on a laptop surroundings body through body I could propose to position an HO textual content someplace at the image

CUTS

Fenerbahce 30 /3

TECHNICAL POINT : The shortest distance among factors is continually a
line, so despite the fact that i draw cuts as curved keep in mind to maket hem
instantly traces as viable while coaching to gamers. Straight Lines are
shorter, and faster. That's why we are saying to "reduce hard"

If an opponent loses you on sight, reducing is a superb idea. If the participant
is popping his/her head to test your area that means, the instant he/she turns
his/her head to peer the ball again, thats the time for a reduce.

Cutting the front of the display screen, or the defender offers you benefit to
put up the participant, and extra smooth passing alternatives to get the ball.

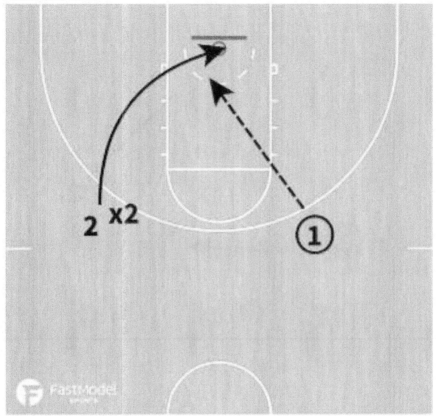

Teach your gamers to backdoor reduce if they're over played(denied) regardless of what. If your participant ratings one in all those, there can be no extra competitive denying.

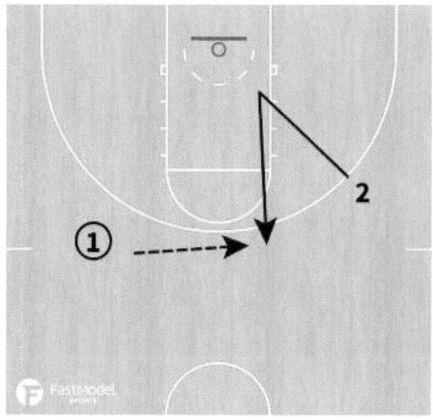

Very essential of clearing out and getting the ball.

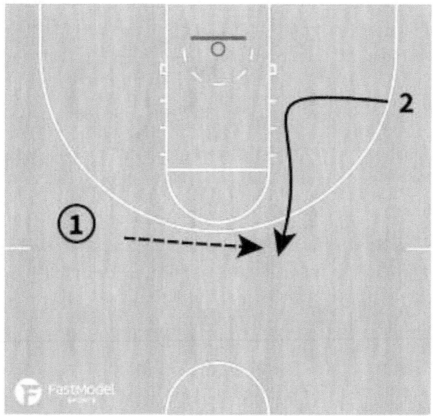

Same concepts with V reduce .

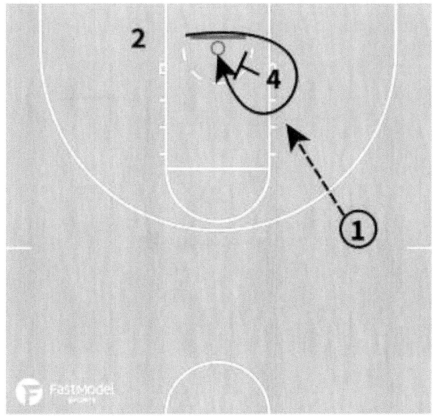

If your defender is following you, A curl reduce is a superb preference to use.

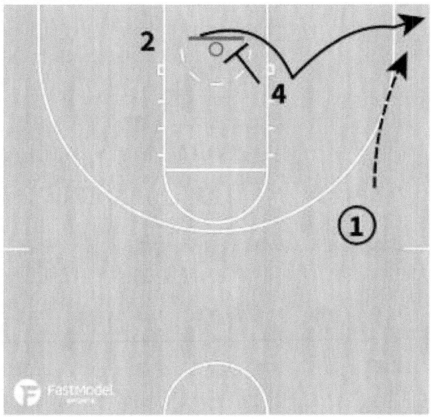

If your opponent thinks he is sensible and lazy, he's going to in all likelihood take the fast reduce. Every try to move below the display screen might also additionally create a flare reduce option. I love this form of returned pedaling cuts.

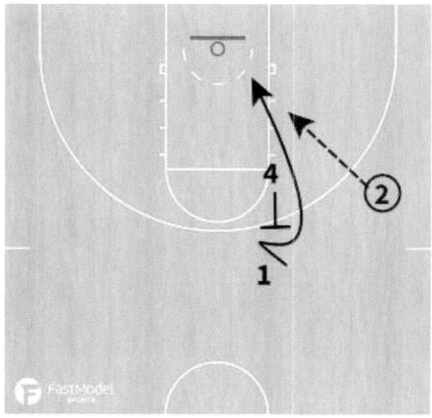

One of the excellent performs in the sport for Give and move

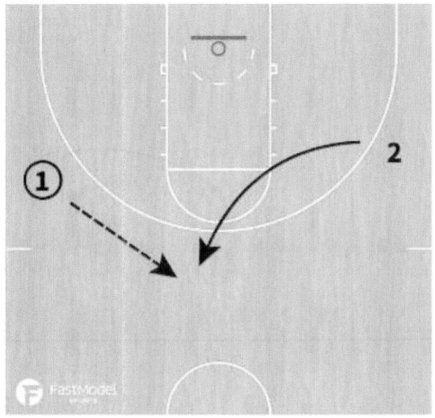

Shallow cuts are the cuts to fill the empty defend spot. It may be from the susceptible wing

Or it may be from the sturdy with relying at the play.

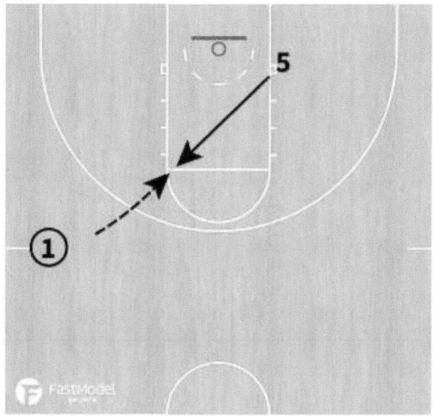

Very beneficial in sector offenses. Getting the ball earlier than the opponent wakes up.

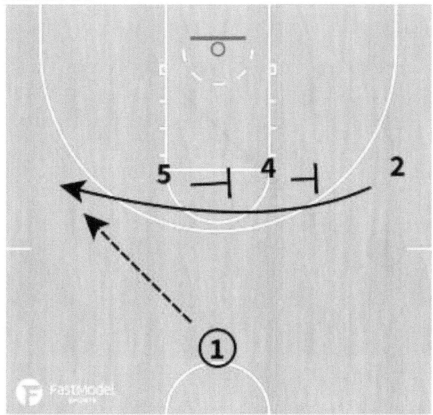

Alon Iverson used those form of cuts, to clean and get the ball. You can play an ISO after this.

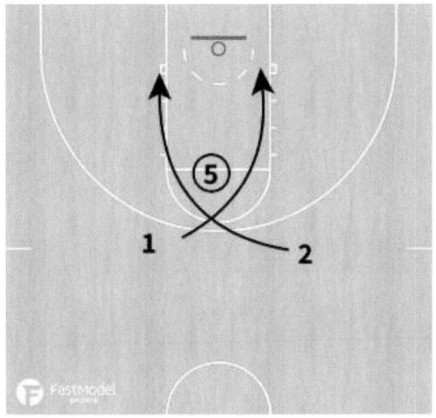

I actually have visible this paintings many times. 1 and a couple of is reducing on the identical time, developing displays for every different as well. Second cutter is maximum possibly to get the ball. Some groups want to display screen for 1 and a couple of, in the event that they don't get the ball withinside the first area and developing every other opportunity.

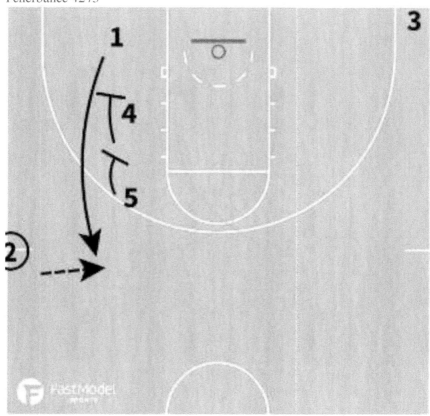

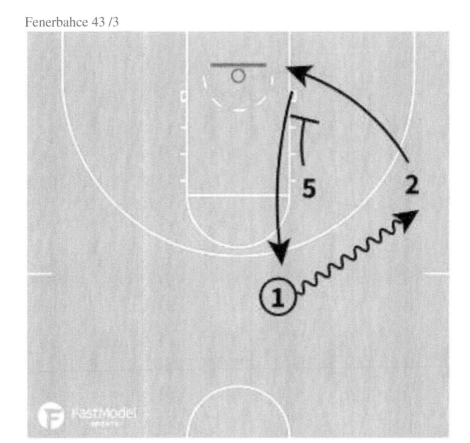

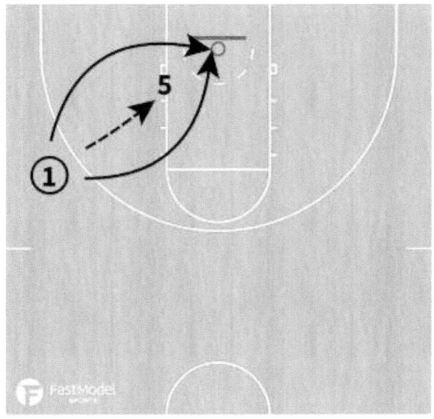

This reduce brings more benefit to the put up participant , on the grounds that there can be no assist on that side. Post gamers must watch for a clearance first to move.

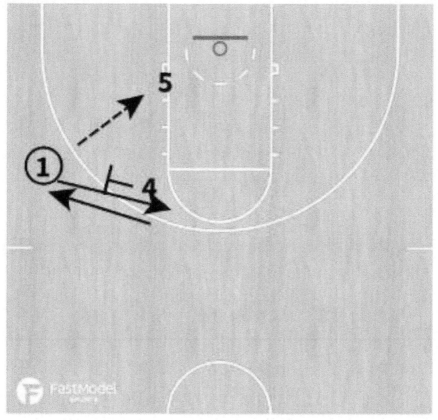

One of the beauties of the set performs with a terrific three pointer. Re-screening is the key.

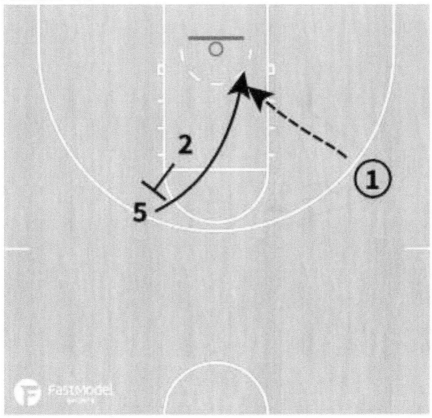

This is one in all my favored cuts nowadays. Post ups aren't preferred anymore through maximum of the coaches, however I trust each one in all them would love an empty put up lay-up, or a mismatched put up up play. This can create those.I propose you to make this displays with 5-1 , 5-2 so if there may be gonna be a switch , odds are can be with you.

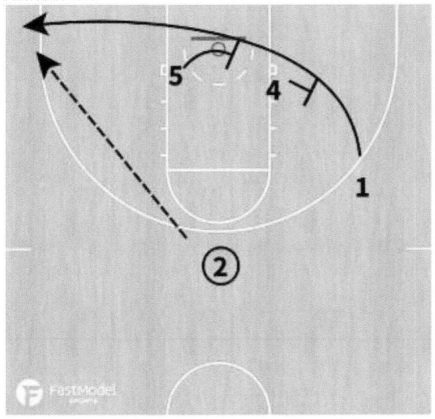

Very powerful towards sector defense, on the grounds that maximum of the time gamers are fascinated with the ball and misplaced song of the gamers.

Fenerbahce 48 /3

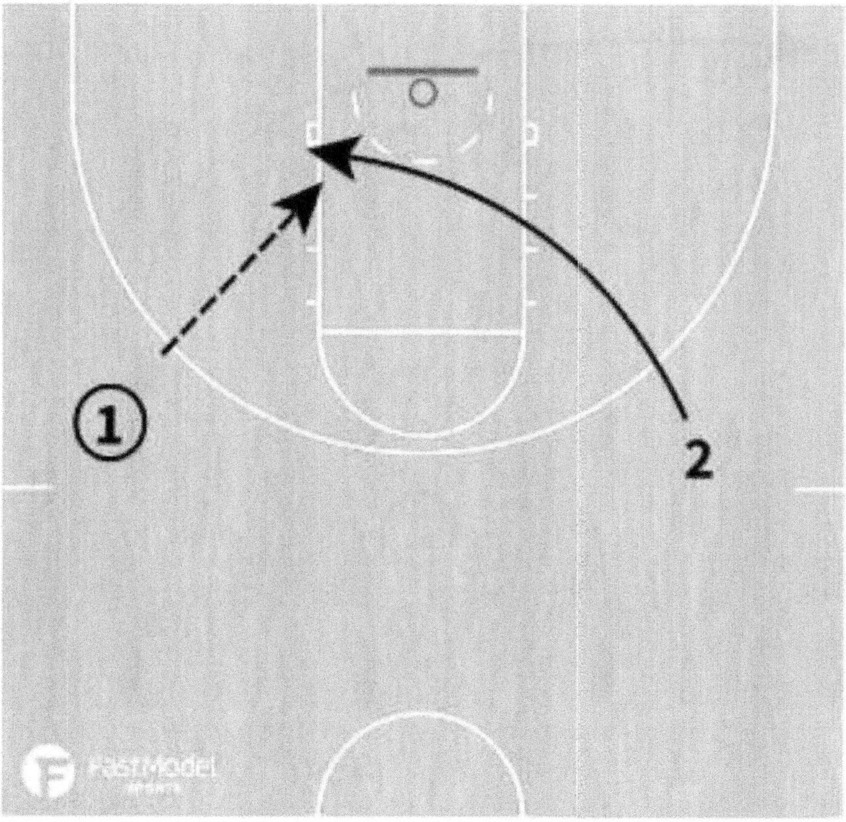

Just watch Warriors and you'll see trillion of examples. The display screen location is probably different , is probably on elbows as well.

https://www.youtube.com/watch?v=6FRikiZXK5U
https://www.youtube.com/watch?v=Wsf7uvl6NhQ

SCREENS

There is a false impression that massive guys need to display screen. Depending what you are attempting to create selected who will make the display screen, additionally we've visible currently that screening "your personal defender" even is probably a part of a play, to make your defender can't cross for a assist. I assume it is a great concept to make display screen performs with 1 and five. When there's a transfer among 1-five the opportunity of exploiting it as length or pace is maximum.

Every crew use those sort of displays , a few human beings name them as pin-downs. If you're a terrific shooter , pin downs are your bff. If you shoot true sufficient you may see the five guys(defense) leaping to assist and depart his guys open in lots of instances.

Overplayed need to constantly be punished,without or with the assist of a crew mate.

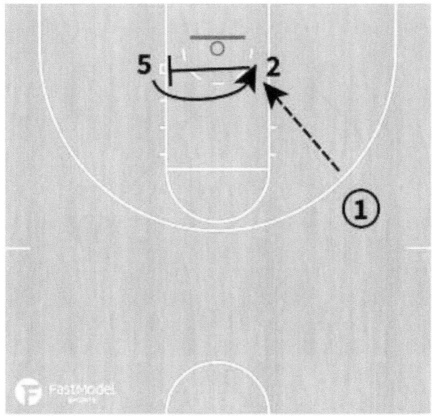

Good manner to begin a submit play. In defense, groups first bump after which observe this sort of displays.

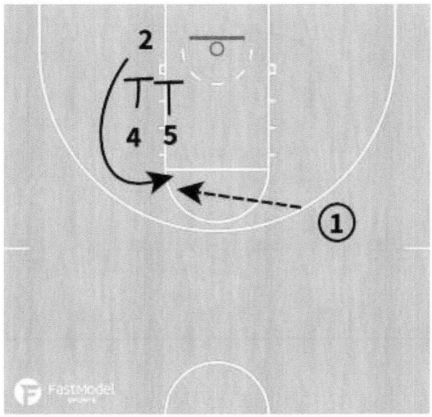

Two Bigs subsequent to every other, one true instance of this sort of display screen is later withinside the ee-e book. Check for "seize the fish" play.

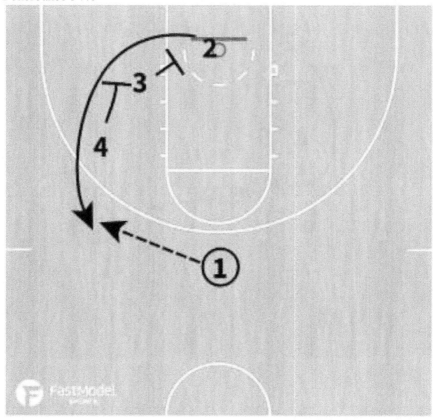

2 displays sequentially used. I actually have visible instances in which three displays sequentially is used as well.

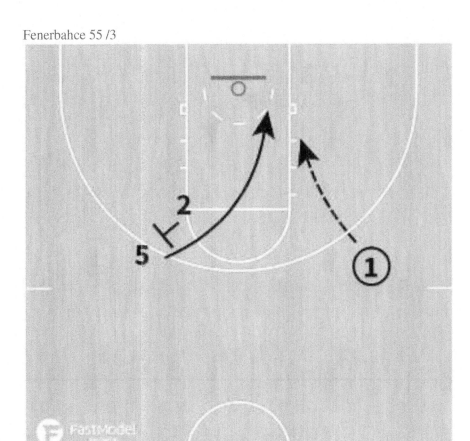

This is my new favored reduce and display screen nowadays. Maybe I am information the price of it currently.

https://www.youtube.com/watch?v=WkcU9d3TNl8

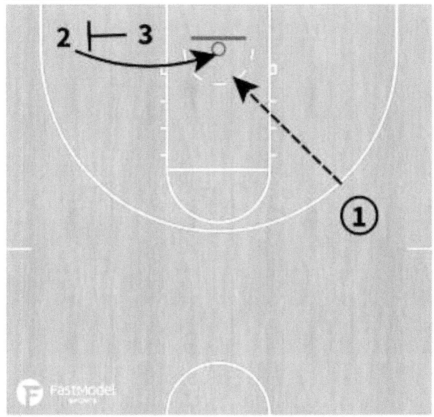

Naming comes from the famous "flex offense" . You can test it later withinside the ee-e book.

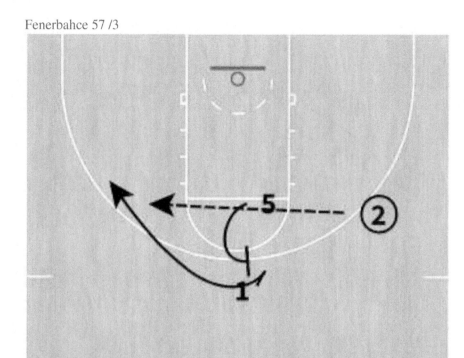

I assume this Is so dope. When I see an elevator play , even they don't discover a opportunity shoot it it makes me so excited. ☺

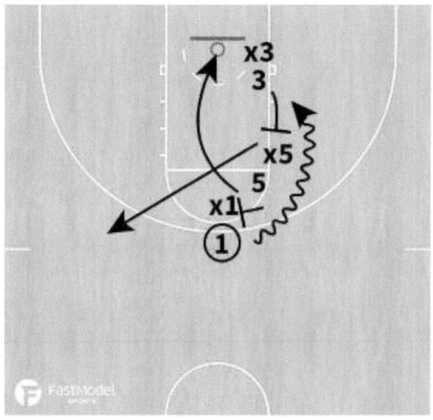

This is referred to as Spain choose n roll. The call comes from the Spanish National crew.. 2 displays manner protecting 2 displays. Without switching it isn't always very probably to be defended.

five displays for 1 this makes defender x5 to reveal up for 1, every other down display screen from in the back of with out being visible takes human beings off shield.five rolling on the equal time it makes it even tougher to defend. And finally three pops out for a 3 pointer.

One of the oldest hints which you need to preserve on attempting at first

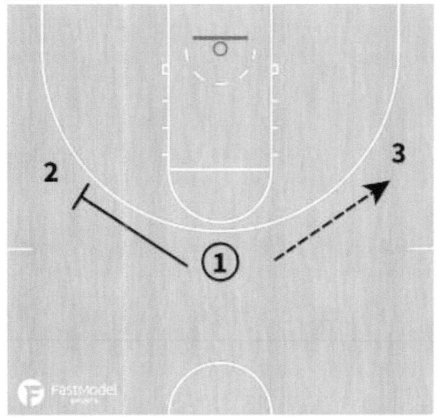

If you don't cross for a ball display screen or a basket reduce , cross for a display screen away. Help a crew a mate. Toss a coin on your witcher! ☺

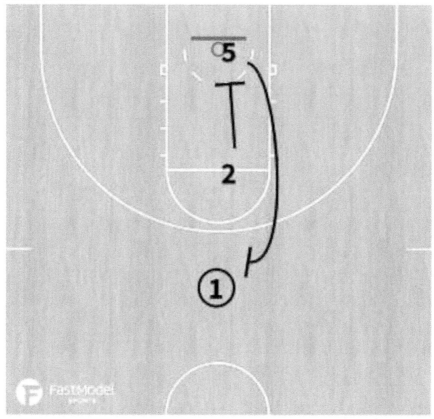

The concept of choose n roll is five(screener) going for walks and creating a display screen. If five can run rapid and make a separation from his opponent that creates drawback for the opponent crew to deal with the situation. For Example : If they plan to double crew it's far now not possible Separation is crucial in choose n roll.

Another transition ball display screen option

Depending at the display screen , maximum of the time five guys rolls four guys pops. Also this double displays maximum probably performed like transition drag displays.

PATTERNS, ACTIONS AND SETS

SET PATTERNS

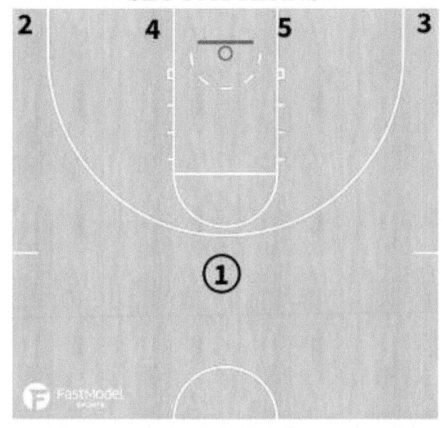

If your shield is right with ISO , this is a great sample. Also short manner to run a excessive choose n roll.

Good concept first of all an UCLA display screen play.

Everybody has a HORNS set. Good spacing , clean availability of displays

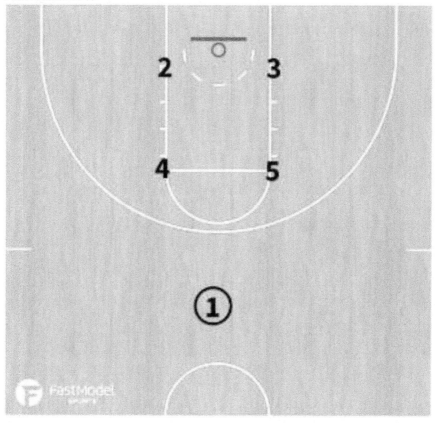

Simple Math : one participant screening out of four he has three alternatives(horizontal, vertical or diagonal) If a 2nd display screen can be performed after this that means three alternatives greater. Making it 9. I like this in out of bounds performs when you consider that it's far symmetric, even your gamers can't visit incorrect places

Cross displays is right for use on this sample.

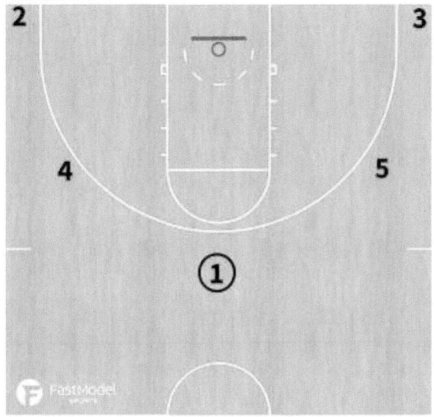

As I instructed you before, 3s are greater treasured in todays basketball, so having crew gamers who can shoot may be very crucial. This kind of sample is more often than not used for movement offenses. Passing and reducing can create double sized gaps to attack.

I actually have a pattern for this , overdue withinside the ee-e book.

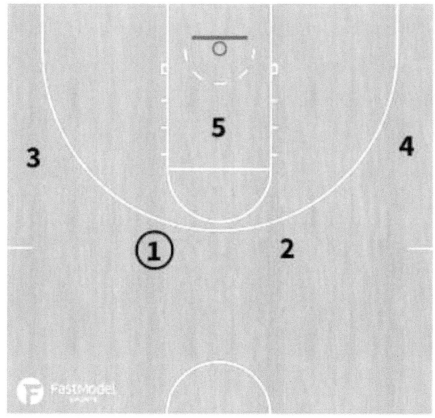

Princeton chin collection is a excellent instance for this sample. You also can play movement offense

Chin Series is to be had overdue withinside the ee-e book as well.

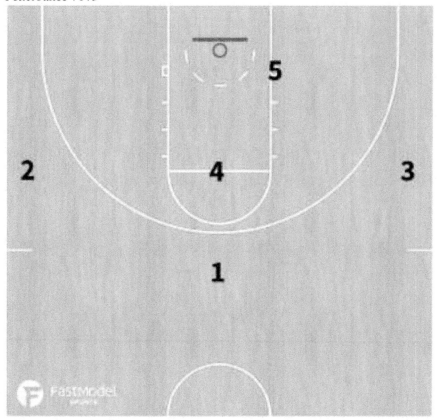

I actually have a terrific transition play for this sample withinside the later of the ee-e book.

Old however gold . This is a keeps play so that you can play this all night time lengthy till you discover a true opportunity. Nowadays human beings strive 2 cuts from this set (1st flex and second down choose)and in the event that they don't discover a gold , grow to be some thing else.

Also to be had overdue withinside the ee-e book.

It took critically many months to recognize the spacing regulations of Side and Top(excessive) choose n roll. Most groups play like this or beneath image.

1-five can roll ,1-four can choose and pop (I assume it's far greater tough to defend, when you consider that we don't realize if he desires to roll or pop.)

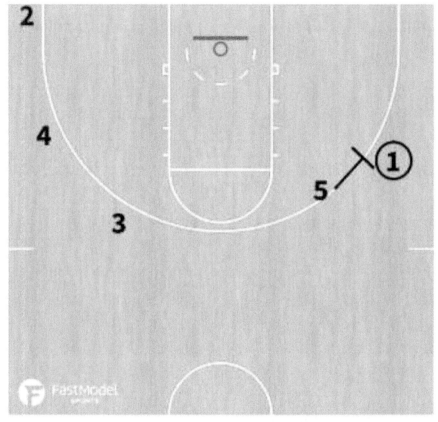

Also three out that means , it's far a three pointer cognizance spacing.

Https://www.youtube.com/watch?
v=aJUIU4K2huA&list=PLQpJzwJlsZfXsBzBzpcBAdzrsl61MWdrt&index=2

I suppose that is the maximum dominant sample in in recent times basketball. Most of the groups play this at remaining ownership of the period, eight seconds left at the shot clock. Switching that is maximum in all likelihood to be punished. But switching at the remaining eight seconds supply gain to protection on time as well.

Short rolls are a distinctive situation wherein the five guys doesn't roll absolutely however brief rolls withinside the center for a mid-jumper or in a assist state of affairs locating the open guy.

manner the ball is dribbled determines the alternative facet to be in assist. They manner the ball is dribbled additionally tells the offense which manner to reduce as well. https://www.youtube.com/watch?v=4CJ3mymG5EY&list=PLQpJzwJlsZfXsBzBzpcBAdzrsl61MWdrt&index=

Shooters dream. All set is performed for you.

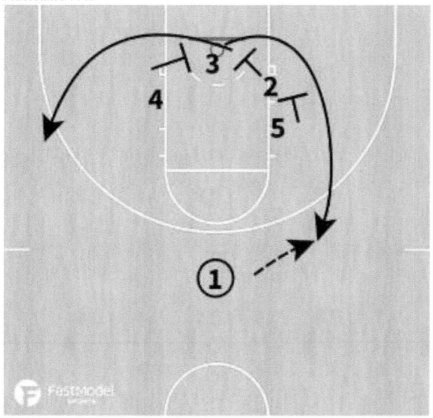

If you've got got shooters, birds with one stone.

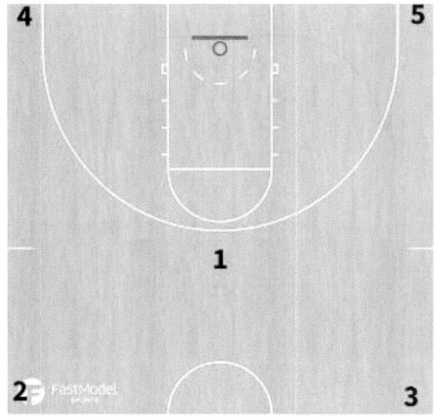

Fenerbahce 78 /3

Very very obsolete sample. This turned into used manner again while there has been no shot clock. Funny that, it's miles now beneficial to transport the ball and spend the time for the remaining seconds with out being fouled.

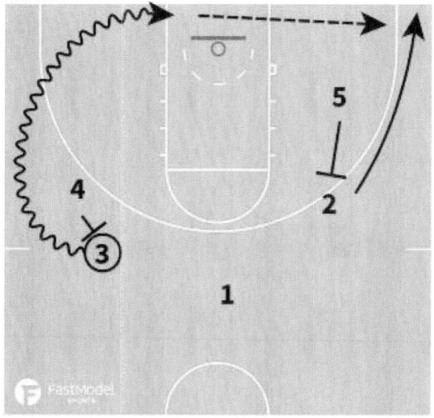

Rule of thumb If there may be a baseline dribble usually placed a shooter at the corner

You can see many spurs units like this.
https://www.youtube.com/watch?v=k5sp6kKSz1s

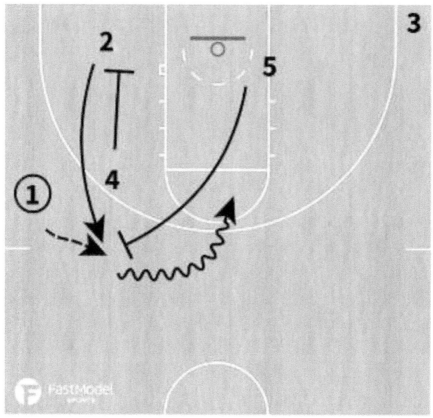

The secret is the timing display screen of the five. Many groups use this as a facet out of bounds play

https://www.youtube.com/watch?v=96iBEZesEUU

this performs is largely 1-2-three passing and handoffing all of the time until a large guy makes a decision to return back and make a display screen.

https://www.youtube.com/watch?v=DEyULvNXBmo

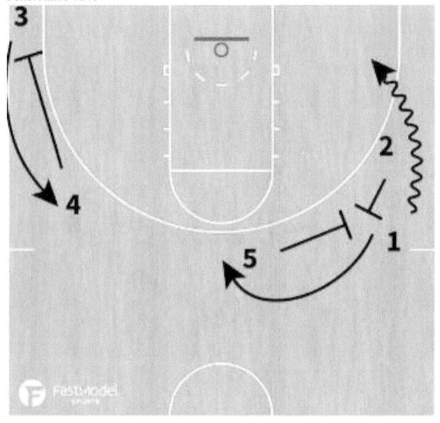

If you want transition basketball that is the concept you should apprehend absolutely . It has many alternatives

- Sending the 1 directly to rim
- Sending 1 to the rim with help of 2 screening , or handoffs,
- if those don't work flare screen by 5 for 2 ,
- if it doesn't work 5 ball screen to 1.

When there may be an motion in a single facet of the ground, It is pleasant to create an motion withinside the different facet of the ground as well. This will make protection occupied with

https://www.youtube.com/watch?v=HiU_xJ_HQV4&t=58s

What we informed before : "over gambling" should be punished. And that is the way you do it with assist of a large.

https://www.youtube.com/watch?v=ZSvZptvUwKg

https://www.youtube.com/watch?v=BmyAPZDHr6E   Simple perfection

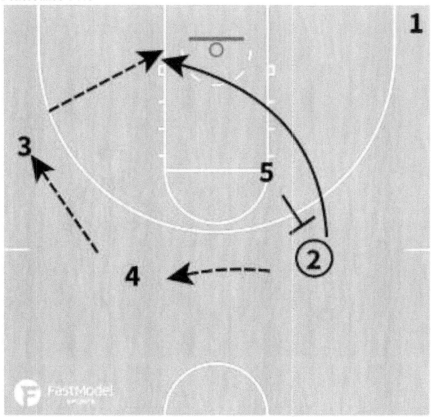

Post up access concept

CONTINUOUS SET PATTERNS

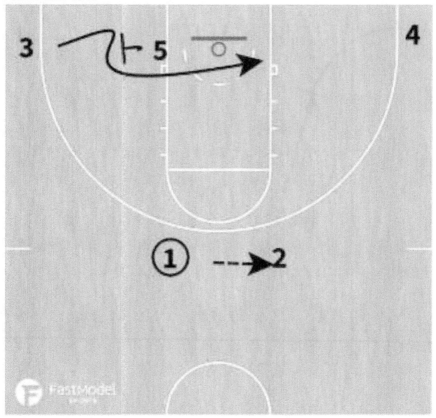

One of the vintage units, however nonetheless used even in NBA. You can see many NBA groups gambling flex offense from a horns set. (At least they may be checking the flex reduce and the after display screen the display screen motion shot)

I suppose flex is a superb set for younger gamers wherein anyone performs in each position.

The set begins offevolved with a lane prolonged byskip from 1 to two . That triggers the five to flex display screen to three. First choice is we locating three for a layup , or a publish up.

If three can't get the ball , display screen the screener motion is called. 1 monitors for five for a shot.

As you may see we've come to the equal positioning as before ,this time overload is at the proper facet.

When 2 passes the ball to five , flex begins offevolved once more from different facet.

https://www.youtube.com/playlist?
list=PLQpJzwJlsZfVvljWOTKgA8cbPF7OH_Vb7

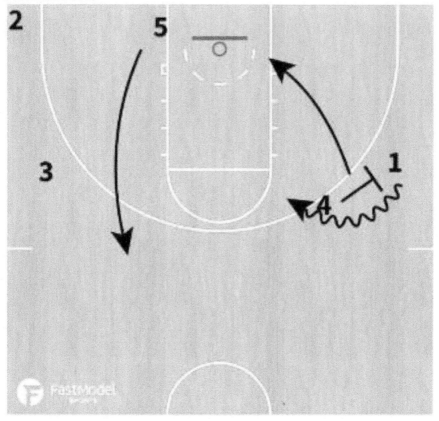

In a few nations that is additionally referred to as Lithuanian Pick and roll. It begins offevolved with a wing select out n roll. As the select out n roll is performed five guy is going high. If we can't locate something at the play the ball is handed to five.

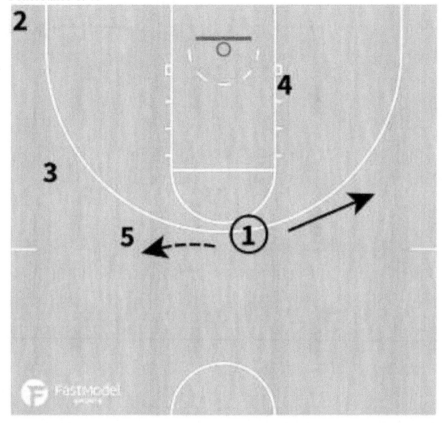

The ball is handed to five. 1 is going to wing for spacing , if he got here too much . four is low at the block.

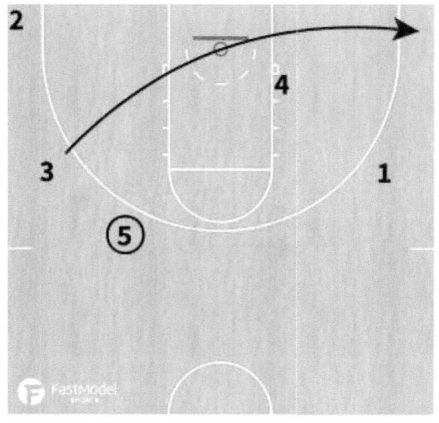

The second five turns in the direction of the three guy , three backdoors automatically (a few different alternatives are there , they may be tweaks , however maximum performed is this) and is going to corner.

three need to be equipped to play now no longer subsequent however the different select out n roll, while the ball is reversed.

five passes to two and , is going for a display screen(If five isn't an excellent passer, Hand off is performed)

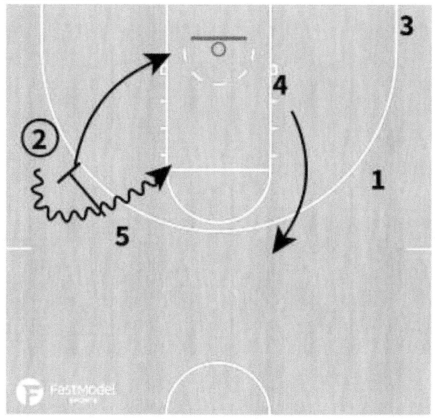

As you may see the equal sample has been reached from the alternative facet. We can once more play this set now.

https://www.youtube.com/watch?
v=CiSVco0OvqI&list=PLQpJzwJlsZfXsBzBzpcBAdzrsl61MWdrt&index=6

Action begins offevolved with a lane prolonged byskip. (You can see a few groups play to 1-three hand off in a single facet and 2-four display screen extrade positions after this they do the prolonged byskip)

And the ball is without delay transferred to the wing. The second 1 passes to three , 2 basket cuts with the assist of five.

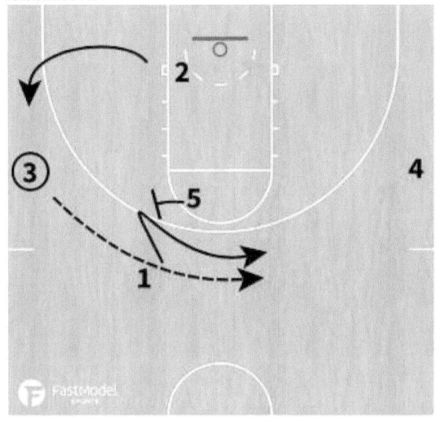

If 2 can't be handed 1 flare cuts with the assist of five. And receives the ball from three.

2 is going to wing and three comes lane prolonged, so the sample is again once more.

https://www.youtube.com/watch?v=NWGtddhRH2E&list=PLQpJzwJlsZfWZhnY7UKZ4XcNcMaFgMhSz&in

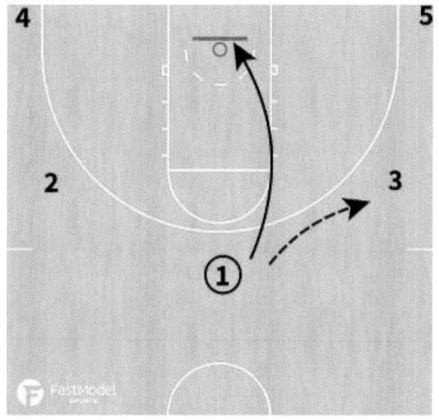

Continuous units concept is to play the equal aspect time and again again, and coming to the equal sample. In this situation I am displaying examples for five out movement offense. The exact aspect approximately movement offense you could usually name the performs as a teach out of doors even on an ongoing play.

First sample is byskip and basket reduce- and fill the ball aspect nook.

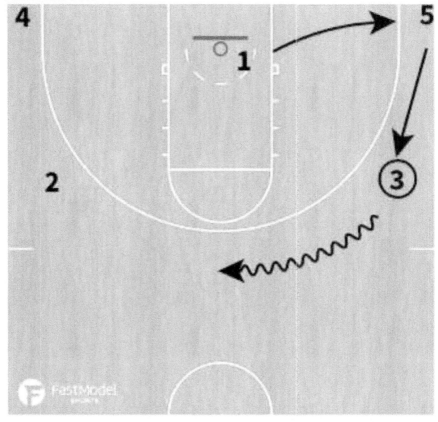

Filling the ball aspect nook is essentially pushing every body to the susceptible aspect. three now has a double hole to assault to his defender.

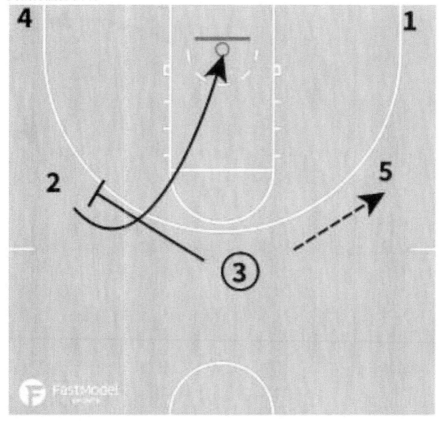

In this situation of five out movement offense : byskip and display screen away, and there may be a basket reduce from the wing.

As withinside the first example , ball aspect nook clearance brings , the ball participant assault to a hole space.

OUT OF BOUNDS PATTERNS

For me , the maximum critical set performs are out of bounds performs. After a ball is out , or a day out has been called , you've got got the time to clean your mind , drop down your coronary heart beat. It is a great exercise to slap the ball while the ball is passed to the participant with the aid of using the referee with a view to wake different gamers.

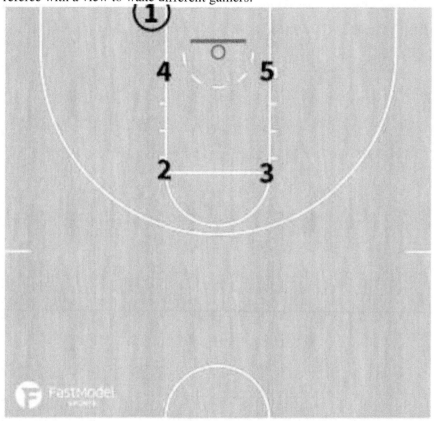

4 gamers in a form of a box. If best certainly considered one among them had a display screen there might be three options. With therefore three extra making nine options.

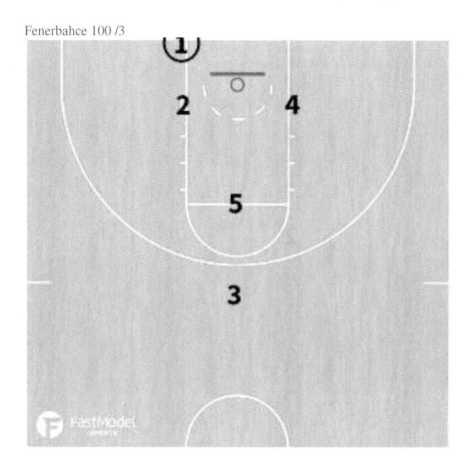

From line , you could speak in confidence to exceptional directions.

Lines are usually approximately opening.

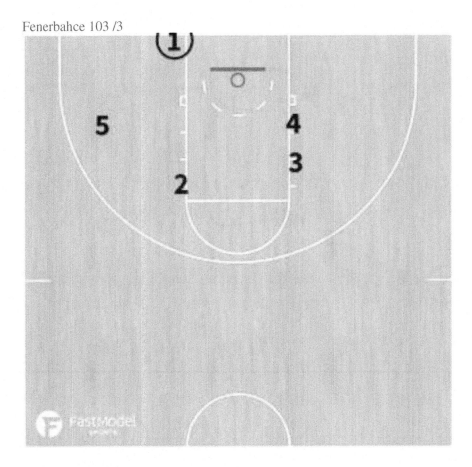

Always deliver a shot choice to 2 .

Teaching factor : 2 Should be under the extent of three . So while he passes shoulder to shoulder with three he may be in lead. If the defender comes to a decision to move beneathneath the display screen , your participant lower back pedal like flare display screen.

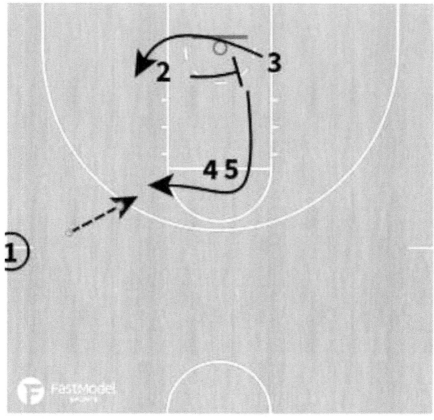

I even have additionally visible this out of bounds play as a transition play as well. (BEAC from Budapest) First choice is publish up. Good spot.

EXAMPLE SETS

OUT OF BOUNDS SETS

5 runs to the nook. 2 in bounds the ball to five. And five passes to three and 1 is going pinnacle of the important thing with the aid of using a display screen, making clean to get the ball. three passes to 1 .

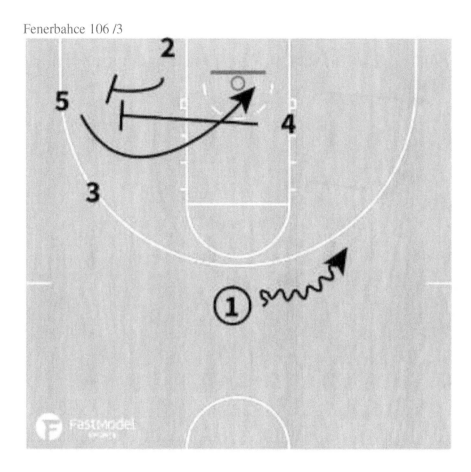

2 and four CATCHES the fish like a net (a double display screen), five cuts for a publish up (into the limited area, if it's miles possible) .When 1 receives the ball he drives left to create a higher passing angle.

Option 2 : 2 is our shooter. 2 runs from monitors for a byskip

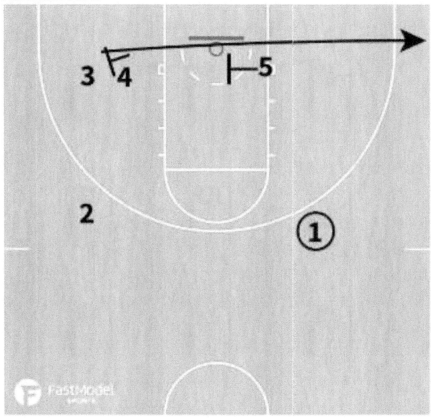

Option three : three is our 2nd shooter and is going to nook for a shoot . five is making a pleasing display screen here. If there may be a transfer five may be used as a publish up again.

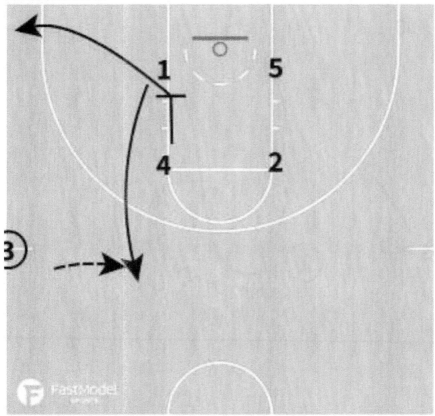

1 comes out of the display screen to take the ball. As he begins offevolved to run the movement on the opposite aspect begins offevolved as well.(Though I didn't display it in this photograph that)

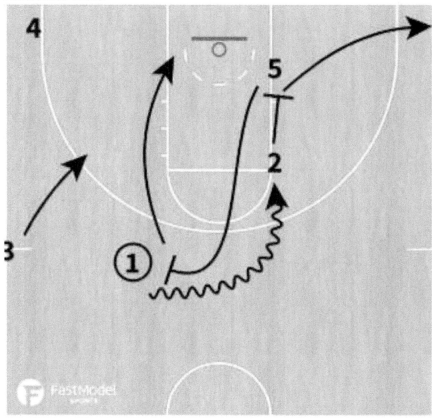

The second 1 touches the ball and sweeps the ball we need our five guy display screen for 1. One of the maximum performed aspect out of bounds play. Every teach have to understand it.

First choice is to discover five open. Most of the time that choice doesn't work. But it have to be examined each time.

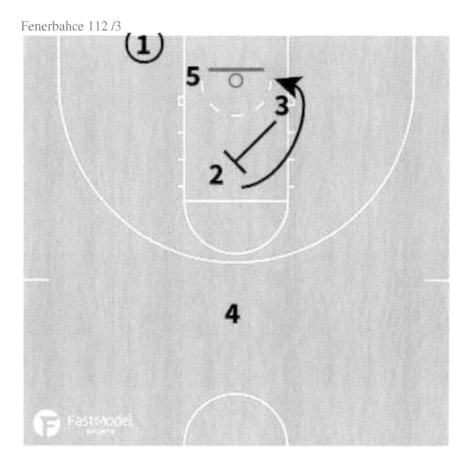

Second choice is two getting the ball . For a layup , or a shot. (Most of the time it's miles a shot) When 2 receives the ball you could play any other set from that factor on.

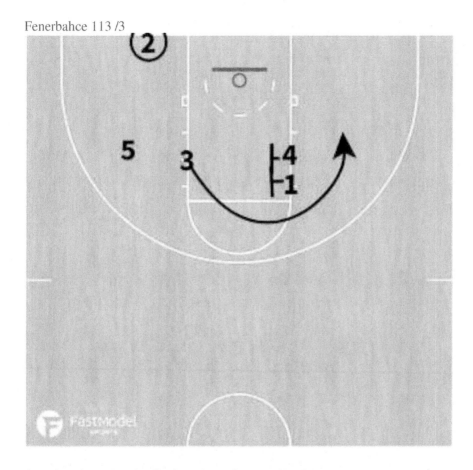

three is going over the display screen for an open shot

If three cannot take the ball , 1 is the second one choice , After the display screen five can move behin the three pointer line so as for any other choice for ball in

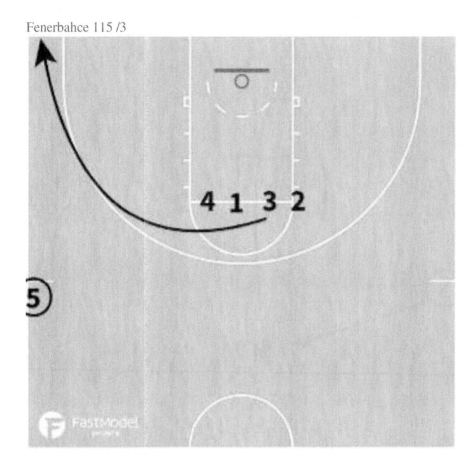

three is opens as much as the nook as a decoy.

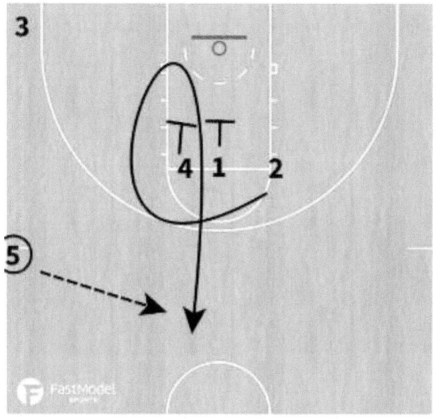

2 makes a curlish reduce after which passes thur elevator doors. This is completed to take the ball in bound.

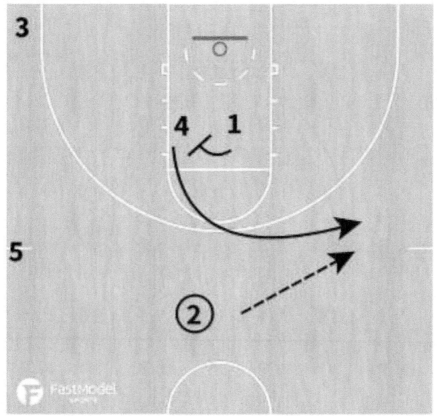

1 makes a display screen four and four cuts to the wing and receives the ball

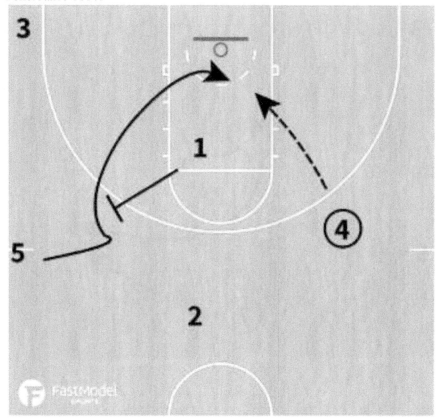

1 makes a shuffle display screen for five. For a publish a play.

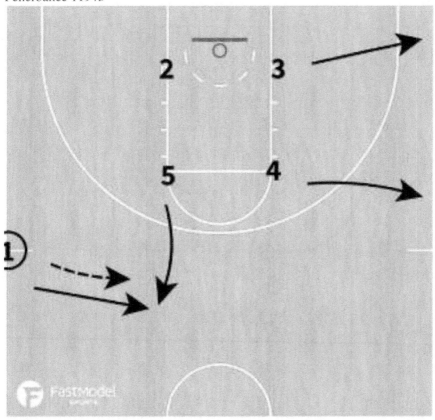

five opens excessive to get the ball and palms of with 1

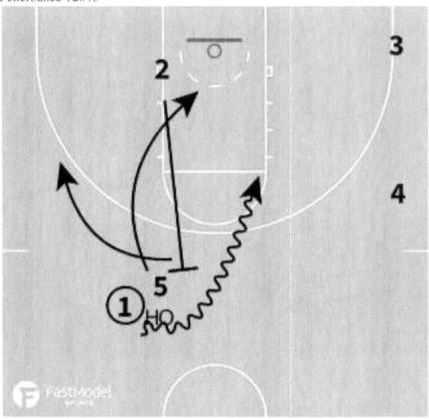

That hand of is likewise a display screen, so 1 dribbles and five rolls , at that second spain choose and roll is performed and a pair of comes for lower back display screen after which is going to wing for a 3 pointer.

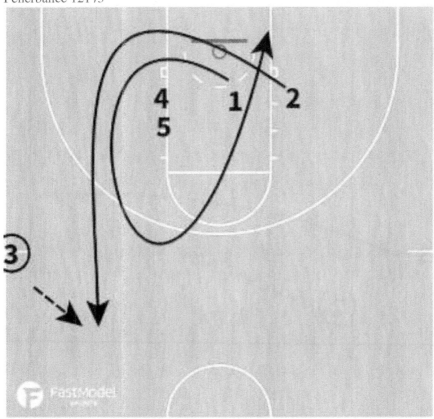

1 cuts first and a pair of as 2nd proper after. four and five stood collectively as a double display screen. Since 2 has reduce proper after that spot might be open while 1 arrives lower back to his spot. So a excessive Lob byskip may be completed as first choice.

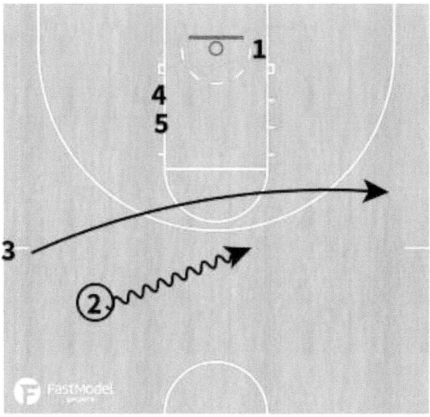

As first choice didn't work , 2 receives the ball and attempts to get withinside the middle of the floor. Where three cuts to the opposite aspect. (We see this in lots of elevator performs as a decoy)

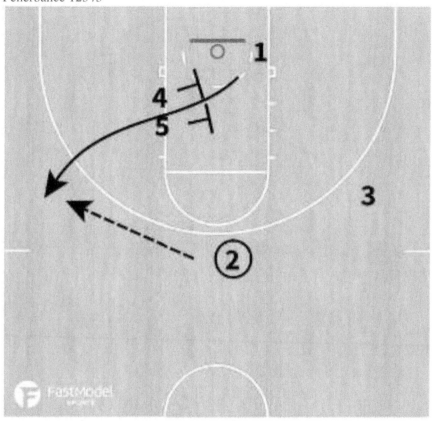

1 is going through elevator doors , and takes the shot.

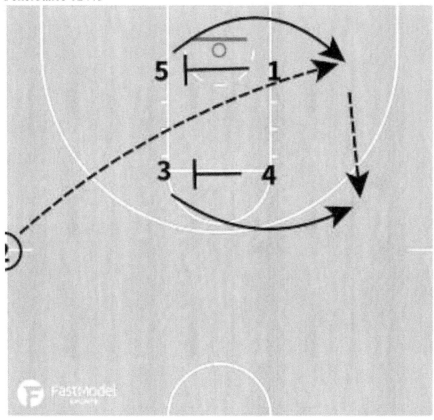

This is a simplified shape of his play. You can see the actual model withinside the clips under.

https://www.youtube.com/watch?v=Wj7IQNCj0iE
https://www.youtube.com/watch?v=mzQG8YBof9c

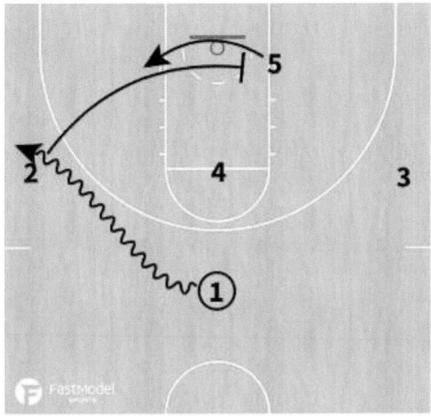

five is in one of the block. Right or left

Guard runs closer to the wing (The choice is : contrary aspect of the five) As the protect runs closer to the ahead , ahead clears the wing move for a go display screen for five.

First choice is five posting up, if that doesnt ocur , four monitors for two for an open 3.

Pass and hand of with quantity four

Basket reduce with the assist of a display screen, and a lob byskip.

https://www.youtube.com/watch?v=ER705pzUvoY

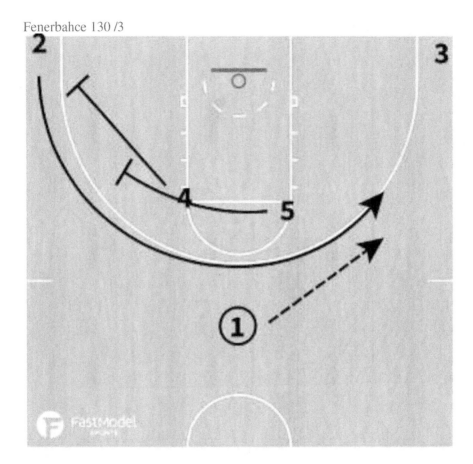

Staggered monitors for two withinside the corner , 2 cuts : it's miles like iverson reduce to the wing to get the ball.

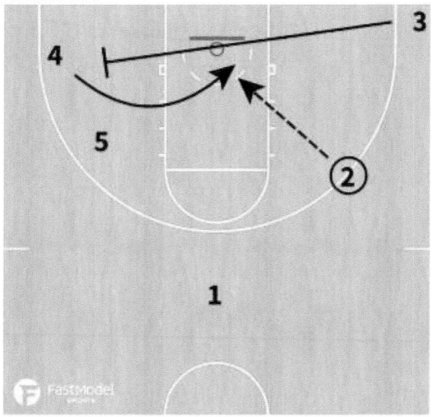

three makes a move display screen for four for submit up.

Some groups use the equal four,five staggered display screen for three to the alternative facet of the floor.

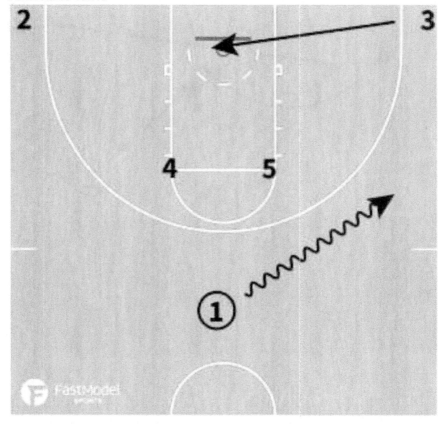

This is one of the simplest and quickest shape of an elevator play. 1 runs in the direction of the participant who may be the usage of the elevator.

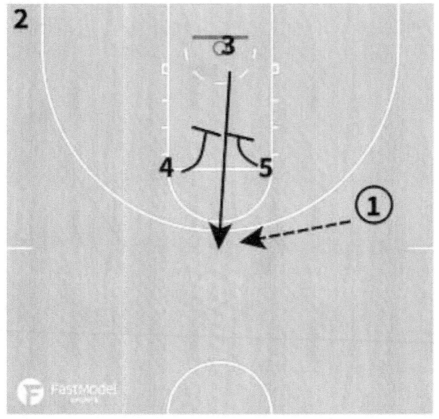

Player runs via the elevator doors. And receives the ball.

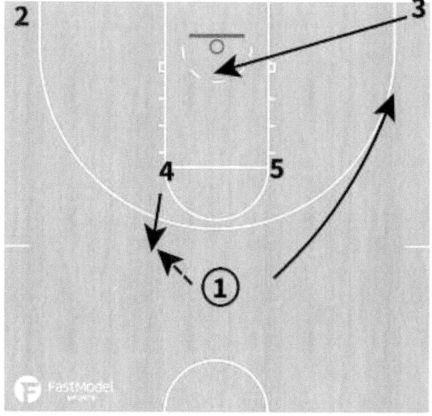

1 passes to four runs to the other corner. This triggers for three to submit up. If he's open we are able to use this.

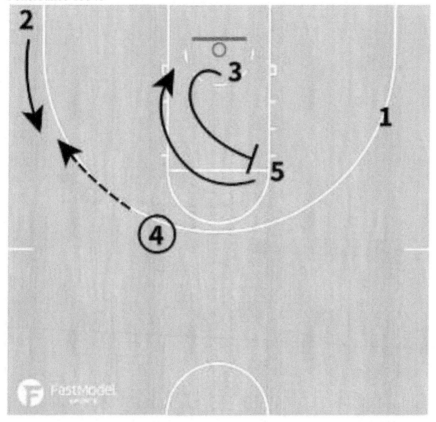

If three isn't always open he's creating a shuffle display screen for five. In the imply time four can dribble or byskip to two, for a higher passing angle.

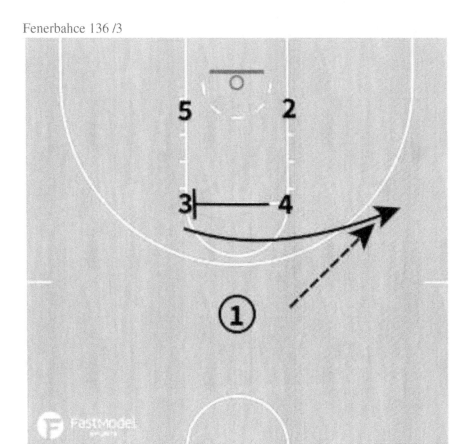

1 passes to one of the open wings.

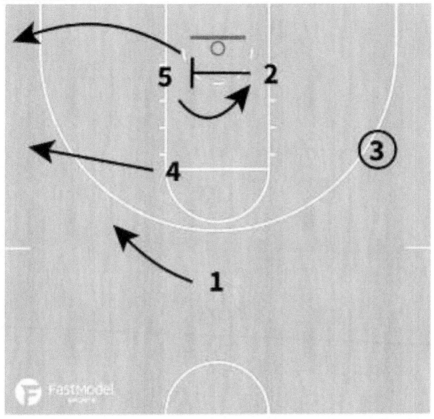

1 runs to the other corner. (To set up ahead choose n roll action) three out spacing or 2 out (corner , ahead) and 1-in quick corner.

2 is going for a move display screen for five. five both can submit up or is going for a wing choose n roll with three.

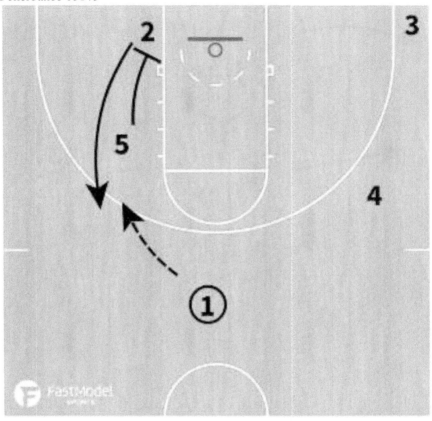

1 passes to two who is going from display screen. After the display screen five runs after 2 (feels like spain choose n roll however it isn't always)

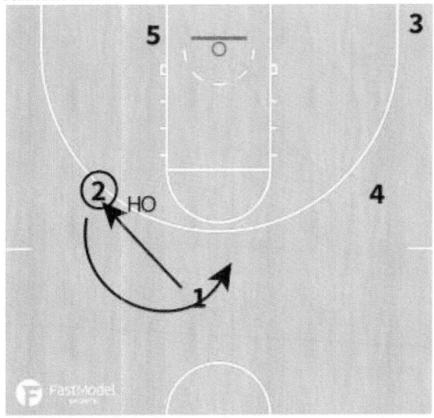

2 passes or Hand off to shut distance 1 . and a pair of actions right.

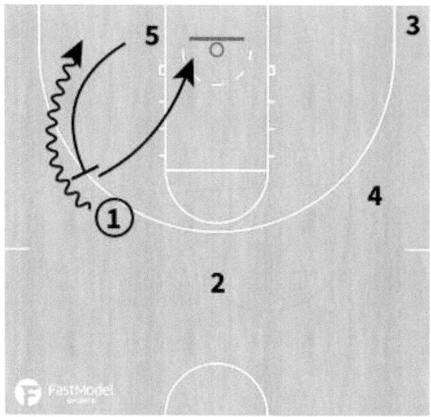

The five guy who screened for two runs and monitors for 1. And performs a choose n roll. This is probably used for a pleasing Hammer action.

Printed in Great Britain
by Amazon

45791289R00081